DISCARD

DISCARD

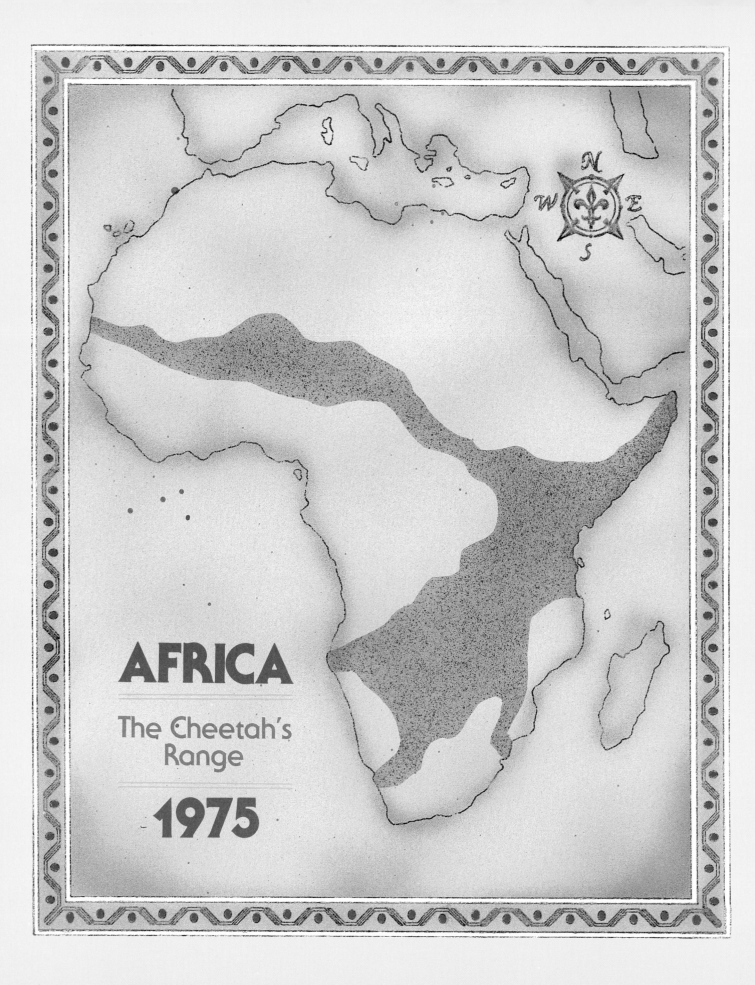

AFRICA

The Cheetah's
Range

1975

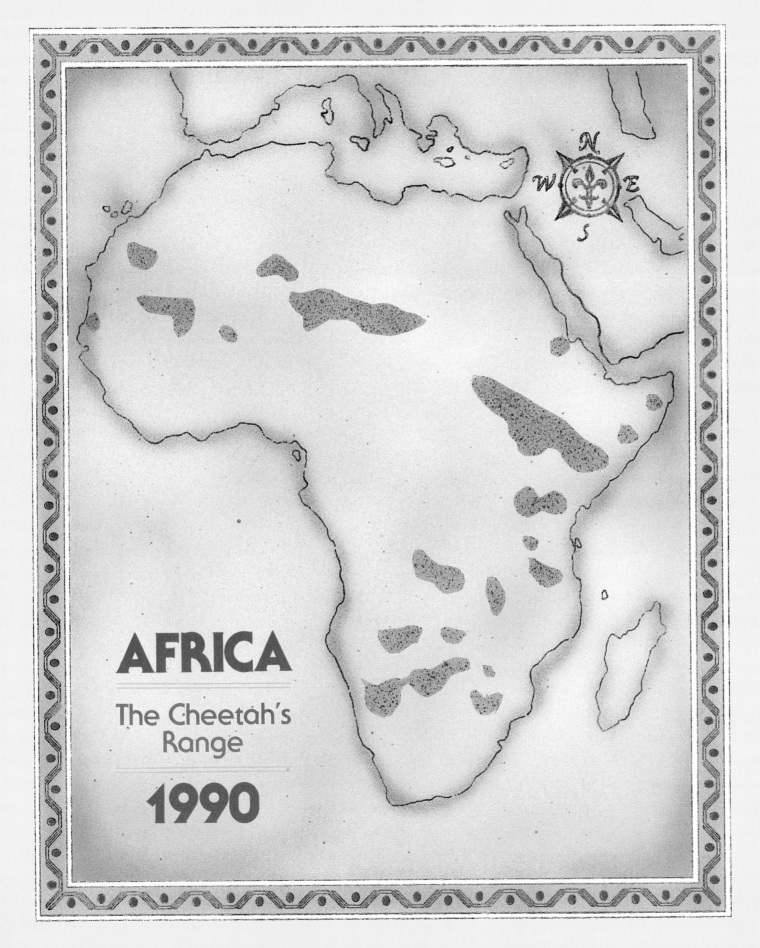

AFRICA

The Cheetah's
Range

1990

A CHEETAH NAMED
ANGEL

DISCARD

BY CATHRYN HOSEA HILKER

A Cincinnati Zoo Book

FRANKLIN WATTS

New York • Chicago • London • Toronto • Sydney

WLS

10/93

J
599.7442
H

TO ALL CHEETAHS, ESPECIALLY **ANGEL,**
A VERY SPECIAL CHEETAH

The author is indebted to Dr. Edward J. Maruska, Executive Director of the Cincinnati Zoo, who supported the efforts to start the Cat Ambassador Program; Barry Wakeman, Education Curator, who offered encouragement and limitless ideas; Chris Kalnow, who always told me, "Don't worry, you can do it." and Frisch's Restaurants, who believed in the program and offered their generous financial assistance to build the "ARC."

Photographs copyright ©: Cincinnati Zoo/Ron Austing: frontispiece, pp. 1, 14, 17, 18, 19, 21, 22, 23, 25 bottom, 29, 32, 33, 35, 40; W. F. Schildman: pp. 3, 5, 7, 8, 9, 10 top, 11, 13, 15 left, 24, 25 top, 26, 30, 31; Paul Silvers: pp. 6, 12, 15 right, 27, 34, 36, 37; Carl Hilker: p. 10 bottom; Dave Jenike: p. 20.

Library of Congress Cataloging-in-Publication Data
Hilker, Cathryn.
A cheetah named Angel / by Cathryn Hilker.
p.   cm. —(A Cincinnati zoo book)
Includes bibliographical references and index.
Summary: A photo essay about a cheetah at the Cincinnati Zoo, who is part of the "Cat Ambassador Program" that sends endangered cats to schools to give children a close-up look at animals that need human help to survive.
ISBN 0-531-11055-9 (library). —ISBN 0-531-15252-9 (trade)
1. Angel (Cheetah)—Juvenile literature.   2. Cheetahs—Biography—Juvenile literature.   3. Zoo animals—Ohio—Cincinnati—Biography—Juvenile literature.   [1. Angel (Cheetah) 2. Cheetahs. 3. Zoos.]
I. Title. II. Series.
QL737.C23H53   1992
599.74'428—dc20   92-14623 CIP AC

Copyright © 1992 by The Zoological Society of Cincinnati, Inc.
All rights reserved
Printed in the United States of America
6 5 4 3 2 1

A CHEETAH NAMED ANGEL

A cheetah lay quietly, but tensely, in the tall, brown November grass. Her color matched the grass and dry weeds around her so perfectly that she was nearly invisible. Her eyes, wide and unblinking, stared into the distance. She listened for a familiar sound. She rose slowly, still staring, then ran swiftly across the grass toward a voice calling her name—Angel.

This cheetah lives at the Cincinnati Zoo, in Cincinnati, Ohio, in the United States. What is a cheetah—an animal from Africa—doing in an Ohio zoo? Why is she important to the survival of all cheetahs?

Angel's story begins over ten years ago.

THE BEGINNING

In 1981 two female cheetah cubs were born at the Columbus Zoo in Columbus, Ohio. The mother of the cubs had never had a **litter** before and she didn't seem able to care for her babies. Many young mother cats, and other animals, have trouble raising their first young.

Zookeepers watched the babies closely for two days. By then, the cubs still had not nursed from the mother, and so they were taken to the zoo **nursery** to be raised there by human beings.

Cathryn Hilker, an animal trainer at the zoo in Cincinnati, Ohio, heard about the cubs at the Columbus Zoo. She asked if she could have one to train and use to teach young people about wild animals. The animal trainers at the Cincinnati Zoo wanted to find a way to give American children a close-up look at the beautiful cats who live with us on this earth.

Cathryn was told she could pick one of the two cheetah cubs. When the cheetahs were ten weeks old, Cathryn visited the Columbus Zoo. In the animal nursery she sat down on the

A cheetah's coat is dotted with dark brown or black spots.
Its tail is bushy toward the end, with a number of black rings
circling it. The tip is usually a bright white.

floor with the cubs. Cheetahs are members of the **felidae,** or cat, family. They belong to the same family as all other cats, including lions, leopards, and the **domestic,** or house cat. But they are different from other cats in several ways. They are tall and slender with very long, delicate legs, and they can run faster than any other land animal. Even at ten weeks of age, the cubs could run very fast.

The two cubs ran and played around Cathryn. They chased each other, hitting one another lightly with their front paws when the chase ended. After a short rest, the chase began again. This is how young cheetahs play in the wild. Finally, the smaller cheetah stopped and stood quietly at Cathryn's side. Cathryn had not touched either animal. She wanted the cats to come to her. Standing next to Cathryn, and purring loudly—sounding like a huge house cat—the cheetah licked Cathryn's hand with her rough tongue. Her tongue felt like wet, scratchy sandpaper against Cathryn's skin.

Cathryn fed young Angel with a bottle.

Cathryn made up her mind. This was the cat she wanted. So the young cheetah, named Maliki, moved from the Columbus Zoo to Cincinnati. She would spend the first year of her life living with Cathryn and her family on a farm near the zoo.

Maliki is a Swahili word, from the language spoken in East Africa where cheetahs live in the wild. Cathryn translated the name Maliki into English, and the young cheetah became known as "Angel."

ANGEL GROWS UP ON A FARM

As a ten-week-old cub, Angel was about the size of a house cat. Her thin, slender legs gave her a delicate look. Her light **tawny** coat was covered with black spots and a row of long white hairs stood up along her back from neck to tail. She would lose this stripe of white hair by six months of age, but as a small cub, she looked a little like a pincushion. Her big brown eyes and the black stripes on her face were just about the only clues that she would one day become an elegant, fleet-footed cheetah.

When she first arrived at Cathryn's house, she was carried into the yard in a large animal crate. The crate door was opened, and Angel stepped out and came face to face with a huge, strange animal. A giant dog, a Great Dane, was staring at her, with his tail wagging.

Dominic, the Great Dane, was a friendly animal. He had been a substitute parent for cats many times before. He had helped raise a lion cub and a tiger cub. During the next week he lay down on the floor—as if trying to look smaller—and allowed the shy little cheetah to explore every inch of his body. Angel did become brave enough to start investigating the dog. Sometimes she climbed up on top of the Great Dane, and walked on him, sniffing him from his tail to his ears.

In time, Angel and the dog became playmates. They played running games, which is what a cheetah does best. Cheetahs are wonderful runners. A racehorse can run 45 miles (72 k) an hour. A cheetah can run 60 miles (96 k) an hour.

Like most baby animals, Angel looked for something warm to curl up near at night. Angel chose to sleep near her human

In time, Dominic, the Great Dane, and Angel grew to trust each other.

Shane, a neighborhood German shepherd, sometimes joins Dominic and Angel.

friends, usually climbing into bed with her **keeper** Cathryn and Cathryn's husband. This closeness caused **imprinting** in Angel. This means that the young animal learned to look on her keeper Cathryn as the **alpha**—the dominant or ruling leader. This relationship between a wild animal and keeper is very important. Because of it, the animal is obedient to the trainer, as it would be obedient to the most powerful, or dominant, member of its **species** if it were living in the wild.

Cathryn spent many hours every day with Angel. When Cathryn was home during the day, Angel always stayed

As a cub, Angel napped as close to her keeper as she could.

where she could see her. This is what baby animals do in the wild. They never stray very far from their mothers. When Cathryn worked in her yard, Angel would lie nearby watching. Angel had free run of a large, fenced yard, where no neighbors could see her.

One day, Cathryn was raking leaves while Angel watched from her favorite spot under a small tree. Lying there, she was well **camouflaged,** and even Cathryn didn't see her. When Cathryn reached down to scoop up the pile of leaves, Angel raced across the yard and batted them out of her hands. Leaves flew everywhere and Angel jumped high in the air,

striking at them with her front paws. She was playing, but in the wild, this kind of play would have been preparation for the serious work of hunting for food. Cheetahs must learn to be expert hunters in the wild by the time they are two years old. They leave their mothers then and must be able to survive on their own.

Angel learned to recognize her trainer's voice and quickly came when she was called. It is important that an animal's trainer be the person who gives it food, since food is part of the reason an animal comes when it is called. Cathryn was always the person to feed Angel.

By the time Angel was one and a half years old, she was nearly fully grown, and weighed 80 pounds (36 kg). She stood 28 inches (71 cm) tall at the shoulder and measured 5 and a half feet (168 cm) from her nose to the tip of her tail.

A cheetah has a short neck and rounded ears. A heavy black line that looks like a "tear streak" runs from the corner of each eye to the corners of the mouth.

Nonretractile claws on each paw help the cheetah grip the ground. The dew claw (see the left paw, above) is sometimes used to catch prey.

Angel had become an elegant animal. She had huge brown eyes, and the unusual black facial markings of a cheetah. Her coat, now the color of an adult cheetah, was light tawny dotted with black spots the size of dimes. Her feet looked much like dog's feet. Unlike house cats, cheetahs have **nonretractile** claws—the claws cannot be drawn back into the paw. The nonretractile claws gripped the ground as Angel ran. Long-legged, muscular, and slender, Angel had the almost magical look of a mature wild animal.

One day, Cathryn brought home a young **mountain lion** named Carrie. Angel and the dog, Dominic, had become good friends, and Angel now looked upon this new arrival as an intruder. She batted the small cat with her paws, but Carrie was a pretty tough creature, too, and she kept trying to get Angel to play.

Angel and Carrie—both now adult cats—take walks together and are still friends.

The mountain lion cub was very small and more flexible than the year-and-a-half-old cheetah. She was able to crawl under the fence and get outside the yard. With the fence to protect her from Angel's fast striking paws, Carrie could play a chasing game with Angel. Up and down the fence they ran until both were tired. Angel soon seemed eager to play with the younger cat, and they often played this running game in the yard. A friendship developed between the two animals. It is a great treat to see animals of different species play together and remain friends into their adult lives.

ANGEL BEGINS HER WORK

When Angel was four months old, she and her trainer started visiting schools, and they still do that today. Angel is the "Wildlife **Ambassador** of Goodwill" for the Cincinnati Zoo. When the United States sends an ambassador to another country, that person speaks for all of us. Angel, visiting schools, speaks for all cheetahs—those who live in zoos and those who live in the wild. When Angel visits a school, her trainer does the talking, but Angel holds everyone's attention. Angel visits nearly a hundred schools in the Cincinnati area every year. Angel has been seen by over one million people. Angel's job is to give American children a chance to see a wild animal that comes from another part of the world and to learn how important cheetahs and other animals are.

All animals are important to our world because they are part of the "**web of life.**" Just as individual threads of a spider web are connected and are needed to make the web hold together, all life on earth is connected to make the earth strong. All life depends on other forms of life to survive. Even worms are important to our world because they help make the earth's soil productive so we can grow food. People are important, and so are the animals that help keep the world balanced and beautiful. If you have never heard of or seen a cheetah, you might not know that now they need help from human beings to survive.

A visit from Angel, the cat ambassador, gives students a close look at
a beautiful, and threatened, wild animal.

Besides visiting schools, Angel has appeared on television. At her first television appearance, Cathryn was nervous, but stepping into the spotlight never seemed to trouble Angel. The "Bob Braun Show," a Cincinnati interview program, was her television debut. The hot lights and cameras didn't bother Angel; she was more interested in the thick, round television cables that lay all over the floor. Whenever a cameraperson moved a camera, and the cable moved with it, Angel tried to grab the cable. Cathryn kept saying "leave it," which is a command that all trained animals must learn.

Since her first television appearance, Angel has been a guest on many programs. She licked David Letterman's hand. She met Bryant Gumbel of the "Today" show. She appeared on "Good Morning America," and on the Cable News Network, and even jumped on the couch with Regis and Kathie Lee on their morning talk program.

At zoo programs, visitors watch Angel (below), the snow leopard (top, right) and the serval (bottom, right) demonstrate their natural abilities and learn about the problems the animals face in the wild.

ANGEL'S POPULARITY

When Angel was one year old, the Cincinnati Zoo had a birthday party for her. A large cake, with one huge candle on it, was placed in front of Angel and everyone sang "Happy Birthday." Angel sat on a chair in front of her cake. When the candle was lit, she hissed at it. That made the candle go out. Everyone laughed and wondered if Angel had made a wish before "blowing" out her candle.

Ten years later, the zoo had another special birthday party for Angel. Her birthday cake was shaped like the earth, and had ten candles on it. This time Angel was more interested in the cake and she took a big bite. All her whiskers were coated with the thick frosting. Many students from schools she had visited sent Angel cards to wish her a happy birthday.

Students who have met Angel at school or in the zoo remember her because they have watched her running in her play yard, or have come face-to-face with her and seen her keen eyes looking far into the distance, or felt her rough tongue as she licked their hands.

Angel's tenth birthday party

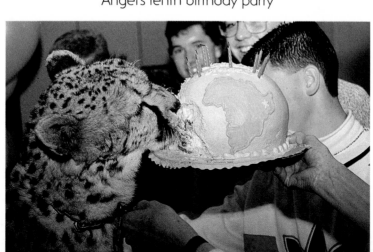

ANGEL TRAVELS ABROAD

As the "Wildlife Ambassador of Goodwill," Angel has been sent on some long trips. One trip took her to Central America, to the country of Belize. No cheetah had ever been in Belize before, since cheetahs are not **native** to that country.

The government and people of Belize have been working to protect wildlife. Some wild cats and other species of animals in the world are in danger of becoming **extinct**—they may disappear from the earth. Cheetahs are one **endangered species,** and the **jaguars** of Belize and Central America are endangered, too. To try to save these big wild cats, an area of land, the Cockscomb Preserve, has been set aside in Belize as a special place where the jaguar can live in safety.

The prime minister of Belize and his children meet Angel.

In the parade through Belize City, an American woman, Sharon Matola, rode on the truck with Angel and Cathryn. Sharon lives in Belize and has started a zoo so that Belizian children can see and learn about their country's native animals.

The preserve is a **sanctuary** for the cats, and nothing is allowed to disturb them in it. Angel was sent to Belize to call attention to the government's work to save its native cat, the jaguar.

A public ceremony was held to welcome Angel, and she appeared with Manuel Esquivel, prime minister of Belize at that time. Newspaper reporters and television crews recorded the scene of Angel climbing a long flight of stairs and standing on a platform with the prime minister and his family.

Angel behaved perfectly as Manuel Esquivel and his family looked at and touched a cheetah for the first time. After the ceremony, Angel was put on a flatbed truck that led a parade through the streets of Belize City so everyone could see her.

People cheered as she sat and stared at the crowds. The children of Belize had never seen a cheetah before.

Later in the afternoon, Angel was driven to a village school. All the children knew she was coming. They had written papers about why wild animals are important to their country. They knew a lot about cheetahs. When Cathryn asked where cheetahs live in the wild, the children knew the answer was "Africa." When she asked what cheetahs could do better than any other animal in the world, all the children in the class answered "Run!"

These Belizian children are getting a close look at an endangered cat from another part of the world.

ANGEL AND HER CAT AMBASSADOR FRIENDS

Angel became so popular that the Cincinnati Zoo found that just one cat could not fill all the requests it received for a wild cat visitor. Even when Carrie, the mountain lion, began making appearances, too, the zoo could not keep up with the demand. The zoo added several more beautiful cats to the program. The first addition was a **serval**—a small spotted cat from Africa—named Missy. Then Tundra, a beautiful **snow leopard** from the Himalaya Mountains of Asia, joined the troupe.

The zoo built a large, special living area for the cats where they could climb trees and run and play. This area is called the "ARC," which stands for Animal Recreation Center. The zoo

Some of the other cat ambassadors: (below) Carrie, the mountain lion; (right, top) Missy, a serval; and (right, bottom) Tundra, a snow leopard

was working to save endangered animals, just as the biblical Noah saved pairs of animals from the flood by putting them aboard his ark. The Cincinnati Zoo and other zoos arrange programs—like the Wildlife Ambassador program—to teach people about endangered animals and what we need to do to protect them. When Angel visits schools, students learn that the cats need help from human beings to survive. Zoo scientists also set up **captive breeding** programs, hoping that animals will produce new generations of species that are in danger of dying out.

Angel has lived at the ARC since she was two years old. All the cats live there once they are fully grown.

Angel, Carrie, and the others are known as "Cat Ambassadors." Each time a school asks for a "Cat Ambassador Program," Cathryn loads the cats in a large van, drives to the school, and presents an educational program for the students. The cats take turns appearing in the programs so they do not get tired or bored by doing the same thing every day. Angel is so popular that most schools request her. All this traveling never bothers Angel. She always seems ready to do what is asked of her.

In the play yard at the ARC, Angel shows how fast a cheetah, the fastest of all four-legged animals, can chase a ball.

A typical school visit for Angel, cat ambassador

ANGEL AND SCIENCE

Every morning Angel is eager to run in her play yard. One day when she was six years old, her keepers noticed that she had no energy and did not even want to get up. It was obvious that Angel was sick. The keepers called the zoo **veterinarian** who took Angel to the zoo hospital so she could be carefully watched. Sick zoo animals are taken to a hospital **quarantine area.** This is a large area with separate spaces for each sick animal. The floor of Angel's space was covered with straw so she would be comfortable. Day after day, Angel just lay quietly in the quarantine area. Her eyes lost their bright luster and her coat became dull. She refused to eat most of the time and grew thin and weak.

The veterinarians performed many tests on Angel to find out what was wrong. They used a needle to take blood from her veins and tested it, just as doctors do when they take care of people.

Angel seemed very sick. Cathryn visited her every day and sat with her. Angel would often lie with her head on Cathryn's lap while Cathryn talked to her and rubbed her body. Everyone at the zoo worried about Angel because there was no clear reason why she was so sick.

Since cats are **carnivores,** Angel was offered different kinds of meat. One day, she was offered freshly cut chicken, just bought from the grocery store. Angel eagerly ate it. This was the first real meal Angel had eaten in a week.

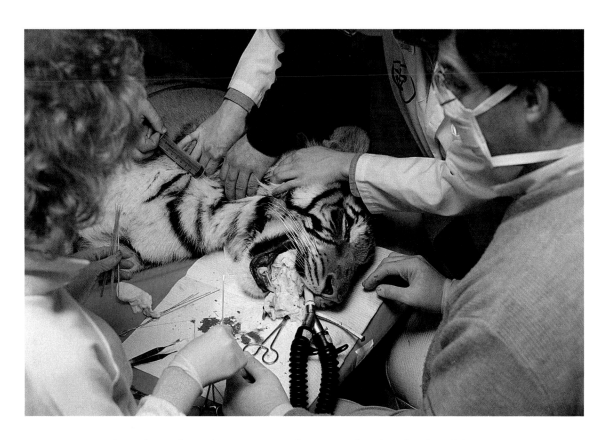

An infected tooth or paw and many other kinds of problems
are treated in the zoo hospital.

For the next several weeks Angel would eat nothing but fresh chicken. The zoo's research department wanted to find out why Angel seemed to feel better eating chicken instead of her regular diet of ground red meat and vitamins. They performed more tests. Cathryn even held a pan under Angel's mouth to collect her **saliva,** so it could be examined.

Finally, the scientists found that her regular diet had too much vitamin A. It was damaging her **liver.** The zoo quickly changed her diet and Angel is healthy again. Thanks to Angel and the research at the zoo, all captive cheetahs now have better diets and may live longer lives.

A healthy adult cheetah—like Angel—is from 30 to 34 inches tall at the shoulder, and weighs from 85 to 140 pounds.

ANGEL—A WILD ANIMAL

So many people have their pictures taken with Angel or have been allowed to touch her, that some think Angel is a pet. Is she a pet? Could she be kept in someone's home, like a big spotted dog? The answer to that is NO! Angel needs her own space and she needs to be left alone a lot of the time. She is not like a dog.

Angel is a trained animal, but she is also a <u>wild</u> animal. She has learned to do what her trainers ask her to do, and she

One of the zoo's popular cat ambassadors is Tiger House Kitty—
the only cat suited to be a pet.

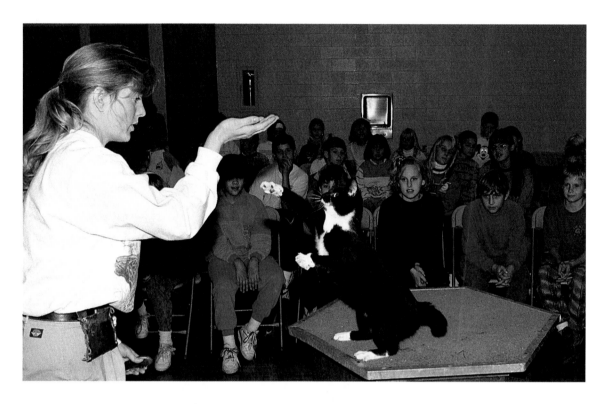

Ambassador Tiger House Kitty performing in a school program

enjoys the attention she gets from her trainers because she knows them well. But there are times when Angel does not want anyone to be around her.

People are not very different from cheetahs in this way. Most people like to touch or hug family and friends, but no one wants to be touched or hugged by a stranger. That is how Angel behaves. She doesn't like people she doesn't know to touch her or give her orders unless her trainer is right beside her to reassure her.

Wild animals are very different from **domestic** animals. Dogs and cats have lived with human beings for many thousands of years. They have been **selectively bred** to be gentle and loving to people. Angel will always be a wild animal, but she is so intelligent and well-trained that she can be used as a teacher so that people who see her will understand cheetahs a little better.

Angel has a special relationship with Cathryn, her main trainer. When Angel was in New York City for a television program, she had to walk down a city street to reach the studio door. Along the way, she crossed over a grate in the sidewalk. Under the grate was a subway tunnel. Just as Angel stepped on the grate, a subway train roared by beneath her feet. She jumped forward, startled, then looked quickly at her trainer as if to ask, "Is everything OK?" Cathryn put a hand on Angel's shoulder to reassure her, and Angel became quiet. It is especially important to have a good relationship with a wild animal if it is going into public places.

ANGEL'S MESSAGE

When Angel was chosen to be the Ambassador of Goodwill for the Cincinnati Zoo, her sister, Sukuri, stayed and grew up at the Columbus, Ohio, Zoo. Sukuri has now raised many cubs of her own. One of these cubs came to live at the Cincinnati Zoo and is being trained to take over Angel's work when she becomes too old to travel.

This young cheetah is called Kenya. He was named for the African country where his grandparents were born. Kenya is now two years old, and he and Angel, his aunt, make many

Cheetahs usually live by themselves in the wild—except as young cubs, when they live with their mothers and their litter mates. When Kenya arrived, it took some time for Angel to get used to him.

public appearances together. They are used to encourage all people to be more caring about wild animals. In Africa, where the last large numbers of cheetahs live, they are considered an endangered species. If we don't protect and help them, cheetahs will disappear from the wild.

Cheetahs need a large area in which to live. They must have space to run and to hunt for their food. When people move into the land and build farms or cities, cheetahs are pushed out. There is less and less space for them. **Habitat loss** is a main reason cheetahs are endangered. Many African countries are now setting aside tracts of land as national parks to provide safe areas for cheetahs and other animals.

Angel and Kenya appear in school programs
and are also used in training sessions for future zookeepers

Even though it is important that cheetahs remain in their native countries, zoo scientists feel that people in the United States must see a cheetah to really understand the animal. This is one reason zoos bring cheetahs to this country. Zoo scientists also hope that captive breeding programs will increase the number of cheetahs in the world.

Cheetahs used to be found in many parts of Asia but, because of habitat loss, they are now found only in some parts of Iraq, Iran, and Pakistan. Africa has the largest population of wild cheetahs. In some places in Africa, cheetahs are killed for their fur. If people did not buy coats made of cheetah and other wild-cat furs, these animals would be safer and have a better chance for survival. Cheetahs raised in captivity are protected from these threats.

Students can help save cheetahs by learning about how these animals live and what they need in order to survive.

And thanks to Angel, the Wildlife Ambassador of Goodwill, cheetahs have a special friend who speaks for all of them, captive and wild.

Coats made of cheetah skins were once popular but, fortunately, we now have laws to stop skins of endangered animals from being brought into the United States.

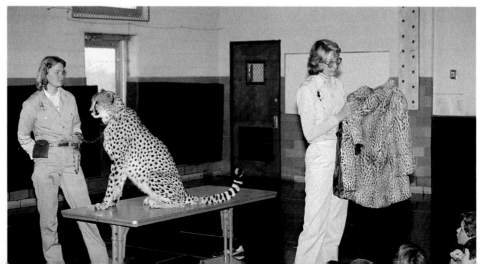

GLOSSARY

Alpha (Al-fuh)—The first, the most important or dominant

Ambassador (am-BAS-uh-dur)—A person sent as a representative

Camouflage (KAM-uh-flahzh)—The colors or patterns of an animal's coat that help it blend into or hide in the natural surroundings

Captive animal (KAP-tiv)—Any animal that lives inside a zoo or animal park

Captive breeding—The planned production of offspring of animals in zoos

Carnivore (KAR-nuh-vor)—A flesh-eating animal

Cheetah (CHEE-tuh)—A long-legged, swift-running, slender, spotted African wild cat

Domestic animal (dah-MES-tik)—An animal that is tame, or adapted to live around human beings and be of use to them

Endangered species—A group of animals or plants at risk of disappearing from the earth

Extinct (ek-STINKT)—no longer living, having disappeared from the earth

Felidae (FELUH-dee)—The cat family, including all wild and domestic cats

Habitat (HAB-uh-tat)—The place where an animal or plant is normally found

Habitat loss—The disappearance of the area that an animal needs in order to survive

Imprinting—An early learning process in which certain animal behavior patterns are established

Jaguar (JAG-wahr)—A large, spotted wild cat originally found from Mexico to Brazil

Keeper—A person who works at a zoo and is responsible for an animal's care

Kenya (KEEN-yuh)—A country in East Africa

Litter —All the offspring of an animal produced at one birth

Liver —An organ inside the body

Mountain lion —The largest wild cat found in the United States; also called cougar, puma, catamount

Native —Belonging to or originally coming from a particular place

Nonretractile claws (ri-TRAKT-ul)—Claws which cannot be drawn back or in (a dog has nonretractile claws)

Nursery —An area of a zoo where young animals are cared for

Quarantine area (KWAR-an-teen)—A place in a zoo where sick animals are kept separate from others to prevent the spread of disease

Saliva (suh-LIE-vuh)—The watery, tasteless liquid mixture produced in the mouth

Sanctuary (SANK-choo-wer-e)—A protected area set aside for animals where they cannot be hunted

Selective breeding —Choosing animals with certain qualities to reproduce. (Domestic cats are selected or chosen to be bred on the basis of a color, size, or temperament thought desirable.)

Serval (SUR-vul)—A spotted, small, 20 to 30 pound (7.5 to 11.2 kg) wild cat from Africa with long slender legs

Snow Leopard —A large, 80 to 120 pound (30 to 45 kg) wild cat from the mountains of Central Asia; has long thick whitish fur with dark markings

Species (SPEE-sheez)—A group of animals that are alike in certain ways. Cheetahs and tigers are two species of cat.

Tawny —Light brownish orange in color

Trainer —The person responsible for teaching animals certain actions (behaviors), such as walking on a leash

Veterinarian (VET-ur-uh-NER-e-un)—A person trained to treat animals medically (an animal doctor)

Wild animal —Living in the natural state; not tamed

FOR FURTHER READING

Adamson, Joy. **The Spotted Sphinx.** New York: Harcourt, Brace & World, 1969.

Carr, Norman. **Return to the Wild.** New York: E. P. Dutton & Co., Inc., 1962.

Harris, John, and Aleta Pahl. **Endangered Predators.** New York: Doubleday & Co., 1976.

Line, Les, and Edward Ricciuti, eds. **The Audubon Society Book of Wild Cats.** New York: Harry N. Abrams, 1985.

Maynard, Thane. **Saving Endangered Mammals: A Field Guide to Some of the Earth's Rarest Animals.** New York: Franklin Watts, 1992.

INDEX

Italicized page numbers refer to illustrations.

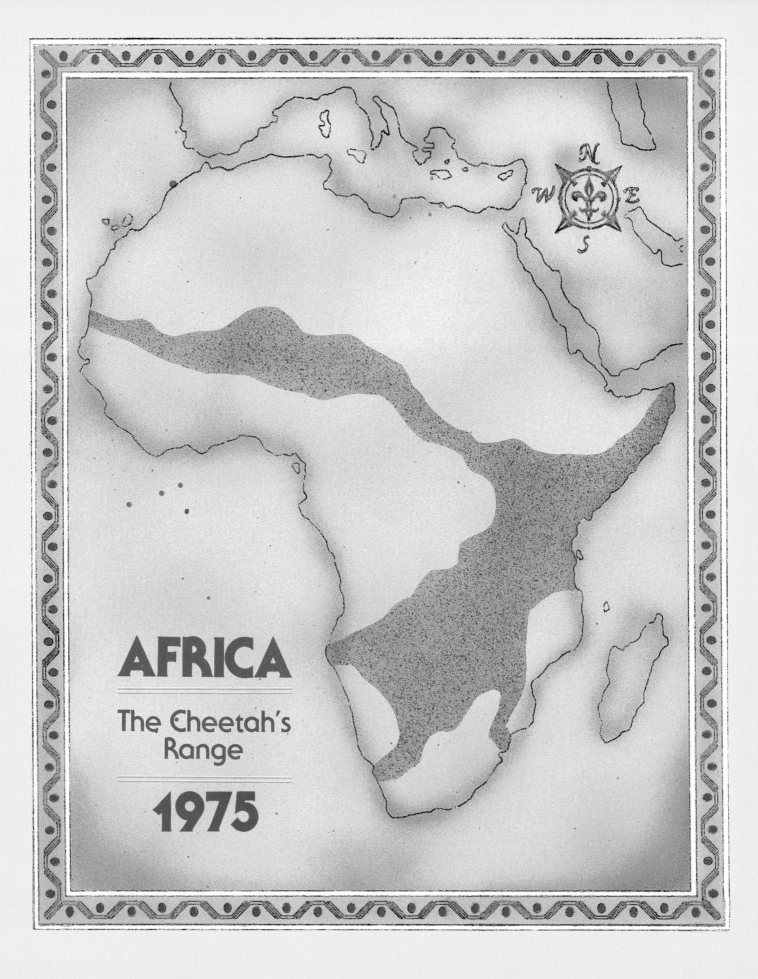

AFRICA

The Cheetah's
Range

1975

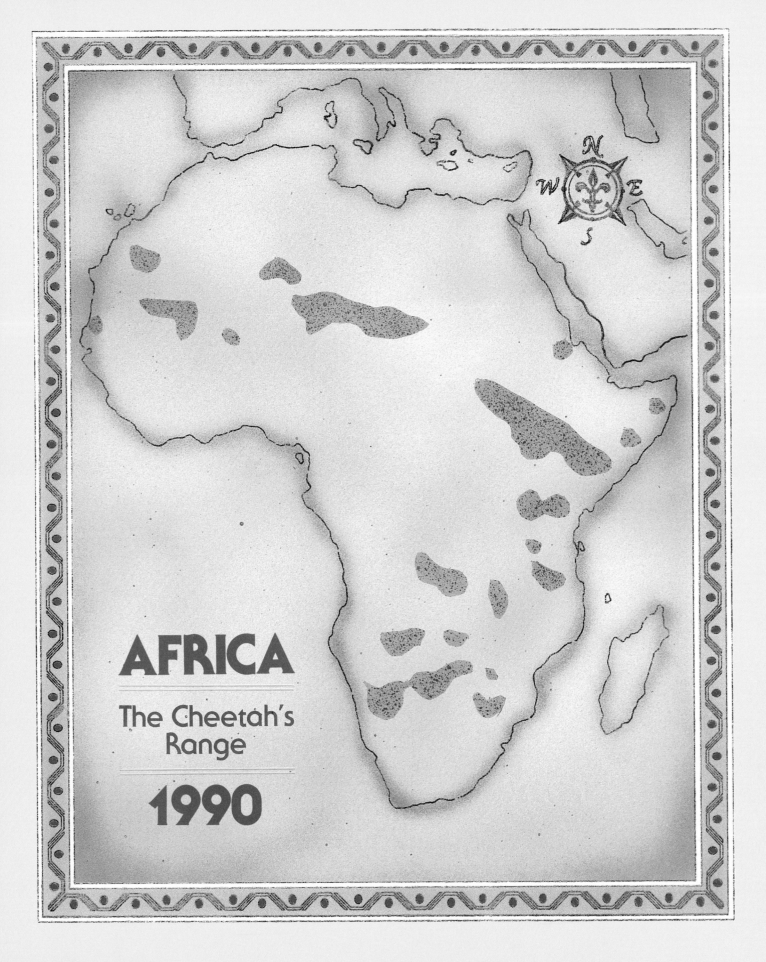

AFRICA

The Cheetah's
Range

1990

J
599.7442   Hilker, Cathryn Hosea.
H   A cheetah names Angel.

DISCARD

DEMCO